BEAUTIFUL GIRL, YOU CAN DO HARD THINGS

HOW TO TURN YOUR PAIN INTO PURPOSE TO COURAGEOUSLY PURSUE THE CALLING ON YOUR LIFE

SLOANE KETCHAM

Leopard Publishing House

For more information, email hello@sloaneketcham.com

ISBN: 978-1-7349077-0-4 (paperback)

Library of Congress Cataloging-in-Publication Data

Library of Congress Control Number: 8737106101

GET THE

You Can Do Hard Things

CRASH COURSE FREE!

As a gift to help you get the most out of this book, sign up for the crash course today! The Course will help you to implement faster, have deeper breakthroughs and crush your hard things with ease!

Crash Course Includes: Audio Book, Study Guide & Mini Course

Sign up by visiting:
www.SLOANEKETCHAM.com/YCDHT

For my daughter, Kaleia
May you always embrace the hard things, knowing that
no matter what - you are loved, you are worthy, you are
appointed, and anointed for such a time as this.

"I can do all things through Christ who strengthens me."

PHILIPPIANS 4:13 (NKJV)

CONTENTS

Introduction

Beautiful Girl, this is the moment I'm supposed to convince you to read my book. Before I get into all the reasons I poured my heart and soul into these pages and why in the world I could ever believe that you'd care, I want you to know that I'm well aware that I don't know your story.

I may not know where you're from or what you've been through. But, I do know we probably have a few things in common.

- Have you ever thought: *Am I enough?* or *Am I worthy?*
- Have you ever had a dream so big, or felt like there was a calling on your life, but you were paralyzed by fear, perfectionism, and/or shame?
- Have you ever been trapped by analysis paralysis?
- Have you ever had an inspired thought in

the shower and swore to yourself and God that you were gonna get after it, but you didn't do anything?

- Are you worried about what other people will think if you tell them the secret dream for your life?

Me too! I knew we'd be fast friends.

To build our connection even more, let's see if this morning scenario sounds familiar.

Do you wake up most mornings, your confidence on fleek, get your workout in before 6 a.m., ideas of epic proportion firing on all cylinders, feeling like a queen? Your kids get themselves up and ready for school, all with smiles. Your email inbox is at zero, and three Instagram stories are posted (#nofilterneeded) as the Rocky theme song plays in the background. And it's not even 8 a.m.!

Girl, seriously?! If that's how your day started, then this book is NOT for you. Let me save you some time, and let's part ways now. No hard feelings.

But, for those of you still here, let's look at another scenario. I definitely think it's more familiar.

You woke up with the hopes of conquering the world,

but instead, your mental list of a thousand things to do took over everything.

Reality set in because it's 6 a.m., and your kids need something. They always need something...

You put on your yoga pants, and that's as close to working out as you'll get today.

Then, you're pulled into the kitchen desperately thinking, *Give me coffee, or give me death. Put it in my veins —straight into my veins.*

The only theme song playing in the background are the notification dings going off on your iPhone.

Does that morning scenario more realistic and relatable?

Here's the thing. We both know that you'll get 'er done. (That's not the real problem, but we'll get to that in a second.) No matter how chaotic life is before 8 a.m., you find a way to make it happen. Fast forward to 6 p.m., and you may need a glass of wine, ibuprofen, and a shower. You flick on a rerun of the *Real Housewives of* somewhere, get into bed, and start your mental to-do list all over again...

So the real problem with this scenario is that you forgot something. Well, maybe you didn't forget it. You just have to scroll down to the very, very bottom of your list to find it.

You forgot to put YOU on your list. Or worse, you put YOUR to-dos on the list, but you feel like you're spinning your wheels, stuck on the woman-who-can-do-it-all hamster wheel of doom.

Allow me to clarify. I'm not talking about exercise, your nails, or waxing something as to-do list items. Your list is missing the YOU stuff that may look a little something like this...

- Write a book
- Write a song
- Design a clothing line for kids, women, or men
- Start a coaching business
- Start a nonprofit
- Launch an online course
- Open a boutique
- Launch a new website
- Start a podcast
- Book a paid speaking gig
- Host a live workshop
- Hire an assistant
- Learn Facebook Ads
- Create a webinar
- Take over the world

The YOU stuff on your list should include your dreams. The vision for your life. The calling that God's placed on your heart that you keep shoving to the bottom of your list. Those are the YOU things I'm talking about.

Over the years, I've accomplished a lot. I have done almost all of those things on that list above and more. I've been an entrepreneur, coach, speaker, and trainer for over a decade. I've coached women (and a few brave men) from all over the world, helping them to do all the things—start businesses, write books, launch courses, etc. And I did this by helping them map it out, so they had specific actions they could take to achieve their dreams!

Action

It's only by the grace of God that I can say I've been blessed to live out the calling on my life, because trust me, I would've never thought this country girl from a town of 3,700 would ever have the kind of peaks and valleys I'll share with you in this book. There are many days that I stop and pinch myself. Don't get me wrong —life is far from perfect. But I am proof that God will use anyone.

Even me. Far from perfect...but perfected by Him.
    I'm just a small town girl from Hawai'i. I grew up in the country. One road in, one road out. My town

had a population of 3,790 people. I had to look that up, and even I was shocked. When Walmart opened in the town thirty minutes away, it was a party. When L&L BBQ opened, they actually sold out of food.

After a decade of coaching women, I found one common truth, the one thing we're all looking for. The common truth wasn't their industry, what stage of their business or career they were in, their religious background, or their socioeconomic status.

The common truth was that we all just want to believe.

We want to believe in ourselves and each other. We want to be able to say, "If she can do it, I can too!"

But here's the thing. Belief isn't enough. We can believe all day. I could've believed all those years as a teen mom, full of shame and guilt, that my circumstances would change. But if I hadn't applied to college when no one believed I could get in, then I wouldn't have gotten that four-year scholarship and then graduated with honors with my Bachelor of Arts in Communications.

In order to do hard things, you absolutely need belief, but it must be coupled with significant imperfect action. The two go together like poke and rice. (That's the Hawaiian equivalent to peanut butter and jelly.)

So I thought, *What if I wrote a whole book on how to get through the hard things so that we all could confidently and courageously pursue the calling on our lives? What if I exposed the ugly truth behind following your dreams? What if a regular ole Hawaiian country girl showed you what I've done and countless others how to turn their pain into purpose?*

My only goal is that you will say, "If she did it, I can too." And then you do the damn thing and inspire another precious soul just like you to act on her dream too.

"You Can Do Hard Things" is not just a pretty Pinterest quote. It's a mission, motto, and manifesto. When you speak those words and then take the steps to actualize the process, you can and will change your life.

Before we get any further, I want to warn you. There are three negative thoughts that might pop into your brain from time to time. They will steal, kill, and destroy the gifts that are waiting for you in this book.

I want to expose those negative thoughts right now because what is in the dark will come to light sooner or later. But now you'll be equipped to stop those thoughts in their tracks.

Negative thought #1: I already know this.

Whenever you think this, I want you to ask yourself: *If I already know this, am I putting it into action?* If you are, then follow the saying: when you know, teach. Ask yourself: *Who can I teach? Who can I help?*

Negative thought #2: This won't work for me.

As soon as this comes up, I want you to ask yourself: *Why not? Why can't this work for me?* What I'm about to share can and will work for your hard things too. I've seen it happen over and over again. I have confidence in you and your ability to be bold and brave in moving forward to accomplish your dreams.

Negative thought #3: She's successful because of her family, husband, and/or education.

This thought is the worst. It's rooted in comparison. As Mark Twain once said, "Comparison is the death of joy." It will kill your joy. Or it'll rob you of even striving for joy. Everyone has a story of how they came to their position of success, and what is seemingly an overnight success story in reality is a ten-year winding-road-with-obstacles story.

There is no perfect moment

You can't wait any longer. That perfect moment that you have in your mind, where you'll go on some magical retreat at a swanky hotel for a week, sip mimosas by the pool with your MacBook Pro and leather bound journal, and finally be able to map out and execute your perfect plan to launch your dreams, read this book—

Yeah, I know. Guess what's not gonna happen.

Even if it does happen, it's never as perfect as it seems.

I've actually done it. Escaped for a week to my favorite hotel, sat by the pool with my MacBook Pro, had a mimosa, jumped in the pool, and decided that I didn't want to work! I wanted to drink the freakin' mimosa and relax.

There was too much pressure.

I know what you're thinking. *But Sloane, if I had some time away from the kids and responsibilities of life, I would 100% get it done!*

Maybe that's true. But I wouldn't want you to. It's more fun to plan a celebratory spa day with your best girls or a staycation at with a guilt-free shopping spree. You wouldn't not have to pick up the phone, check email, or worry about what's happening on the business front.

Trust me—I know!

I'm going to show you an excuse-free way, full of ease and grace, that does not require you to lock yourself away to accomplish your dreams. 'Cause girl, You Can Do Hard Things!

This book is meant to be read over and over again. I kept it short and sweet. KISS, or "Keep it simple sister," is my motto. It's also meant to challenge you. And it's designed so you'll think of me as your coach, not your cheerleader. Although, I do have some cheerleader-like tendencies, and I may know several football cheers by heart.

Here's the thing, I'm a self-diagnosed workaholic, often obsessed with success at all costs. I love designer bags, I only drink great wine, and I love Jesus. But I swear, I yell at my kids more than I'd like to admit (never the dog, though), and I go to therapy more than I go to church. *What is wrong with me?!* I guess I'm a walking contradiction, and I'm okay with that!

I believe this book found you, mama. There's some nugget in here that you're gonna walk away with. I don't know what that'll be, but I know it to be true. And if you want to better your odds of getting the most out of this book, science has proven that people remember 10 percent of what they read, 20 percent of what they hear. So read and listen at the same time, and according to my math skills, you'll retain 30 percent.

Before we continue, I want to make another point that I'm an imperfect Christian. I talk about God, and if that offends you, then we can part ways now. My hope is that it won't, but it's okay if you have to go. I call Him God, but you may call that spiritual guidance in your life the universe, Jehovah, or Buddha. No matter what word you use, the principles in my book will work for you! I know they will. I know it because over the years, I've personally mentored and coached women from all walks of life and from every religion.

This book is a call to action for all women to rise up no matter your spiritual beliefs, where you were raised, how much money is in your bank account, or the circumstances of your current life!

The chapters are organized by some of my life's hardest things. They are hard things that most women go through, and they've been some of my most teachable moments. I then share with you my *You Can Do Hard Things Fail-proof Formula* to conquer any and every hard thing. Whether you want to start a business, or just be a better you, after years of failing forward, I found a better way, and I'm so stoked to share it with you.

My hope is that this book will help you to courageously pursue the calling on your life, that it will inspire you to take significant imperfect action, and that it fill your heart with a whole lot of faith. I am here to tell you that the seemingly impossible is possible.

Again, I don't know what you've gone through, but I'll bet that what you're supposed to do with your life, and I'm not talking about moneywise. I am, however, talking about your purpose and mission in life. The lack of action are tied to moments of hesitation, frustration, or your darkest pain.

That thing that happened to you does not deserve the power to define you. You Can Do Hard Things. You can turn that pain into your purpose.

But sister, I'm also here to tell you that it's not going to be easy. I did manage to figure out some things along the way. I've unpacked my process of conquering the hard things in life, and I'm super excited to share them with you in this book.

My path from pain to finding my life's purpose and calling has been the hardest thing that I've ever had to go through. To really help someone, you have to be willing to truly heal from all your pain first. It's only then that you can sit in someone else's poop and help them turn it into manure.

Are you ready? Of course you are! The rest of this book will help you navigate through fear and pain and not enough-ness to become a woman who is ready to take significant imperfect action built on unshakeable faith and certainty.

Let's go do hard things!

Xo,
   Sloane

P.S. Don't forget to claim your free access to the *You Can Do Hard Things Crash Course* at http://www.sloaneketcham.com/YCDHT.

The One Thing

THAT YOU ABSOLUTELY
have to do to
TAKE ACTION ON YOUR CALLING IS TO

Accept it & Embrace it

EVEN WHEN IT'S BORN OUT OF YOUR PAIN.

CHAPTER 1:

You Were Born To Do Hard Things

"The two most important days in your life are the day you are born and the day you find out why." - Mark Twain

I DRANK TOO much wine last night. Who starts a book with a sentence like that? This girl! I also didn't brush my hair this morning. I didn't brush it yesterday either. My 13-year-old daughter stole my car last month—I didn't even know she could drive. My 15-year-old marriage is in recovery, which implies it was previously broken. All I ever wanted in life was to make a living as an author, speaker, and coach. And it's what I do every day. Yet, there are so many moments I feel totally overwhelmed and overworked.

. . .

Ever feel like life is kicking you in the balls, laughing at you, and kissing you all at the same time? I'm writing a book about doing hard things, which would have you think that I know how to do hard things, and you would be correct. But the irony is that in order to write a book about mastering the hard things in life, you have to have gone through them and know how to embrace them as they thrash about in your world.

Most people think I'm naturally outspoken, a born leader, the first to raise her hand in class. The truth is I am now, but those skills didn't come naturally. I learned developed those skills myself. In reality, I was the girl who sat in the back of class using my long hair to hide myself. I was shy and felt unworthy. I was awkwardly tall, growing up in Hawai'i where a girl's average height is 5'5", I was 5'8" by sixth grade. Literally the tallest girl in the entire school, adults included. Besides Mr. Thorsen who was a giant.

For the last ten years, even though I've been helping countless other people get after their biggest dreams, I've struggled from time to time to get after mine. It was as if everyone else deserved to live their dreams, but for some reason, I had to sit in the back seat. Like my dreams weren't that important. I battled what I call Mommy syndrome.

. . .

Mommy syndrome is highly contagious and spreads rapidly when you find out you're pregnant. Symptoms include:

- guilt when you want to do something for yourself
- decreased exercise
- fatigue
- frequent irritation with your spouse or partner
- decreased alone time to do things that make you feel good (think massages, spa days, and endless mimosas)
- tendencies to put your dreams and ambitions on the back burner

Listen sister, it was a major feat to even finish this book. But I was not about to let Mommy syndrome get me down again. I was determined to finish it. I knew I had a message, a calling, and I had to answer it.

Your calling

There's a difference between a calling and a thing on your ever-growing list of want to-dos. If you've ever wondered what your calling is, ask yourself these questions:

- Do I have a dream that's HUUUGE? So big that when I think about it, it terrifies me?
- Is there something that has been on my heart and just won't go away?
- Is this the thing that sparks immediate thoughts like, *Who am I to do this?* Or *I'm not qualified to do that.* Or *Someone else is already doing it,* yet you still can't share it?

If you answer yes to any or all of these questions, THAT thing is your calling. Eureka! You found it!

I had to navigate a long road to accept my calling, but it's always been there. There's always been that quiet voice, and it's still faint even now. But it's there. I bet if you get still enough, put two feet on the floor, grounded and planted in your truth, you'll hear yours too.

For me, that voice is God. Don't get hung up on the term. You may call it the universe or source—it doesn't matter. What matters is that you listen to that voice.

Most of the people I work with know that they want to

help people. They want to take what they've learned, and that often means turning their pain into their purpose. The problem is summoning the courage and navigating the path to actually pursue their calling and turn it into a career.

Pursuing your calling means showing up in this world in a way that will undoubtedly challenge you, and especially those around you. Going after your dreams will be lonely at times, and probably totally uncomfortable. And I'm not just talking about uncomfortable like "being outside your comfort zone." I'm talking about jumping off a fifty-foot diving board kind of uncomfortable.

But guess what, Beautiful. You were made to do hard things!

My mom would always say to me, "Sloane, why do you always have to learn the hard way?!"

As a young girl, I didn't know how to answer that question. I didn't know any other way to learn. It was my nature to figure things out on my own. I was born this way, with a fierce sense of independence and strength that came from the depths of my soul, and resilience that breathed fire.

· · ·

God made me this way because He knew that I would face things in my life that no child, young girl, or woman ever should. He knew that I'd take all the hard things and with His hand, turn them into a life of service, resilience, and healing for myself and dare I say thousands of others.

The one thing that you absolutely have to do to take action on your calling is to accept it and embrace it, even when it's born out of your pain.

All my hard things

I went to Catholic school until I was in the fifth grade. I fell in love with praying and baby Jesus. I learned all the prayers and about all the saints. In first and second grade, I remember being quite obsessed with saints. They inspired me because they all had one thing in common—they helped people who were in need, hurting, or sick. They stood up for people who couldn't stand up on their own...for girls like me.

I wanted a saint of my very own. I wondered if there was a master catalog where you could order the one you wanted, each saint categorized by their strengths. This one's good for travel, this one feeds you when you're hungry, this one is for protection, on and on.

. . .

Back then, Trolls were popular—you know the dolls with crazy pink and yellow hair. I imagined my saint would be just like a travel-sized Troll, and I'd carry her around in my Jansport backpack. I'd give her a cute name like Poppy, and she'd sing sweet songs to me while I went about my day.

Unfortunately, Poppy never showed up for me. I was about four or five years old when my older cousin started sexually abusing me, and I didn't have the vocabulary to ask for help. I didn't understand what to do with the shame and guilt and dirtiness I felt inside.

Statistics tell us that 1 in 9 girls, and 1 in 53 under the age of eighteen experience sexual abuse or assault at the hands of someone they know. Ninety-three percent of perpetrators are family members or close friends.

1 in 9 girls.

It's worth repeating to draw attention.

That means that the odds are that you have been sexually abused, or you know a sister, friend, cousin, or co-worker who has. This is NOT okay. This is an epidemic. I don't know how to stop that. I'm not an expert in that arena. But what I wanna tell you is that this was one of the hardest things I've ever had to face, and I know that I'm not alone. I want to tell you that although my imaginary Troll, Saint Poppy, didn't show up for me when I was a little girl, I found a way to heal and turn all that pain into my purpose.

I thank God my parents put me in that Catholic school. I know they sacrificed a lot for me to go there. We didn't have tons of money, but somehow they made it happen. My mom was pregnant with my sister at the time, and we lived in the country, almost 1.5 hours away from this school. I remember my mom, driving in traffic, eight months pregnant in a tiny Toyota pickup with no A/C.

I thought, *If Poppy wasn't going to show up, I would figure out a way.* So I became the unofficial health room aid in the second grade. Whenever anyone was sick or hurt, I would volunteer to take them to the health room. It made me feel better. It helped me to forget about my own pain, so I kept doing it. There was a period of time I was convinced I'd become a nun, but my emerging fashionista just couldn't reconcile the outfit.

. . .

My mom, like every other Asian mom, was convinced I'd be a nurse or better yet, a doctor. But I hated blood, so that didn't work out.

This calling to help others evolved, and eventually lead me to what I do today. And I'll be the first to admit that the pursuit of my calling has been one that I've wrestled with time and time again.

The misconception is that once we find our calling, it's going to be easy. A sigh of relief. A moment of clarity and freedom. But what I've found is that stepping into your calling and following through on that calling is often the hardest thing.

Your calling is often born out of your pain

About eight years ago, I published my first book, *Living in Your Light*. I was naïvely excited. In the book, I shared in-depth about my battle with depression, suicidal thoughts, and the sexual abuse I'd survived. I was invited to speak at an event for women in need after my book launched. There were about 500 women in the room, and I shared from my book and gave an uplifting message, much like the one in this book.

. . .

As I walked back to my seat, a young girl stopped me, tears streaming down her face. I was scared, a weird reaction as I think back now. But I wasn't prepared for her. She told me that her auntie made her come to the event. She told me that she had reluctantly agreed and had decided that once she got home, she would kiss her 3-month-old son, and then kill herself. But because of my talk, she decided that she had more to live for. I hugged her tight while fighting back my tears. I told her simply that she was made for more, she was important, and that one day, she'd take this pain and turn it into her purpose.

My intent was to stay for the rest of the day, but I just couldn't bare it. It was as if all the hard things came rushing back to me. I got into my car and was overwhelmed with my emotions. *This is what I was called to do, so why did it hurt so much? And if this is what it feels like to pursue my calling, then I'm out. No thank you! Where was this pain coming from?*

And as I made my way back home, the long drive back to the country, I got it. Like a strike of lightning, it hit me. I had to do the work.

You need to do the work

What's the work, you ask? It's simple. The work is fully committing to my own internal healing.

At that point in my life, I hadn't fully committed. I was just getting momentum on my speaking and coaching business, so the last thing I wanted to do was go to talk therapy. I was still operating from my childhood health room monitor days. But deep inside, I knew that if I wanted to serve others at my highest capacity, I needed to help myself first. You know, that whole put-on-your-mask-first thing.

Instead of burying my pain and feeding off the help I wanted to give others, I needed to focus on my healing. So I set out to do the work. I hired counselor after counselor, and professional development experts. I read all the books, but I didn't just read—I consumed and devoured the information like a kid who loves cake. I went to seminars, jumped up and down, sat in contemplation, and journaled in a hundred journals.

All of that to find this one Truth (with a capital T), this one thing that would change the trajectory of my life. I realized that no matter how many books I read or conferences I attended, no matter what kind of physical or material success I had, no matter what morning routine I followed or mantra I repeated—none of that mattered if I didn't feel worthy of it all. So I set out to discover my worthiness. And in doing so, I found my faith.

I encourage you to put in the work and do the same. Discovering your worthiness will empower you in amazing ways.

YOU ARE WORTHY OF

ALL THE DREAMS

PLACED IN YOUR

HEART.

YOU ARE WORTHY.

YOU ARE ENOUGH.

CHAPTER 2:

You Are Worthy

"When you get to a place where you understand that love and belonging, your worthiness, is a birthright and not something you have to earn, anything is possible."
- Brené Brown

ACCORDING TO GOOGLE, the word *worthy* is an adjective meaning

"having adequate or great merit, character, or value."

When I was reading that definition, I wondered who or what determines worthiness. Sure, worth can be judged by degrees, expertise, and initials after a person's name. But internal worth, where does that come from? How do I muster up feeling worthy enough to go after my dreams? How do I eradicate the question, "Who do I think I am?" from my mind forever.

And then I realized, over the years, time and time

again, it's impossible. Yet, I also realized exactly what I could do. Whenever those creepy evil words slip into my mind's eye, I can drop-kick them with this: "Who am I not to...write this book...build this business...lose 10 pounds...have a healthy marriage?!" You fill in your blank.

Listen, the Pentecostal girl in me is about to unleash some love. No one but God defines my worth, and sister, the same is true for you too! In His eyes, you are worthy, period. You are worthy of all the dreams placed in your heart. YOU ARE WORTH IT!

Worthy, but not easy

That's the catch—worthy, but not easy. One of my favorite stories in the Bible is of a woman named Esther. If she were alive today, we'd be fast friends, I'm sure of it. She is simply aaaa-mazing! An orphan sent to live in the king's sex slave dungeon, she was so gorgeous the king chose her to be his queen. She suffered years of abuse and agony. Then, once she was placed on the throne, her uncle (who BTW put her there in the first place), writes her a letter and basically tells her that he needs her to save all the Jews! Yup, *P.S. Save us all.*

Okay, so it didn't go down exactly like that. I'm not a

pastor, so I encourage you to open the Bible to the book of Esther and read it for yourself.

So she's like, WHHHHAAAT?! She tells her uncle to have everyone fast and pray. After the three days passed, she sums up her strength and reconciles her worthiness. She approaches the king, comes up with a great plan, and ultimately, the king stops the execution of the Jews, and she saves her people.

The famous line from Scripture, from Esther 4:14 is:

"For if you remain silent at this time, relief and deliverance for the Jews will arise from another place, but you and your father's family will perish. And who knows but that you have come to your royal position for such a time as this?" (NIV)

(I love that she has her own book, BTW.)

In my years of working with women, a lack of worthiness seems to be the one thing we all have in common. It can be disguised as comparison, a fear of failure, or even a fear of success. It often can show up in multiple forms of self-sabotage.

. . .

When we deny our worth, we deny those who are tied to our indecision to do what's right.

Imagine if in that moment, Esther had decided to not answer her call. An entire population would've been killed. I love this story because it reminds me that the call on our lives isn't for us. It's not for me. Your calling is not for you. The pain you've had to survive has a purpose. Your worth is not defined on Google or by other people. It's defined by what you are willing to do.

Are you ready to answer the calling on your life? Are you ready to step into your worth? I hope so, 'cause we're waiting for you!

DO NOT
LET YOUR
CURRENT

circumstances

DEFINE
YOUR

future

CHAPTER 3:

It Starts With YOU

"You drown not by falling into a river, but by staying submerged in it." - Paulo Coelho

I USED to love watching gender reveal parties on Instagram. You too?! NO? Okay, I guess it's just me...

One night, red wine in one hand, phone in the other, I must have spent a solid hour scrolling through the search for #genderreaveal. That's when I knew I had a problem, and it had to stop.

Let me explain. 'Cause I bet I sound like a crazy lady at this point.

I had my oldest son, who at the time of this writing is 21, when I was just 16 years old. There were no parties. Okay, well, there was one baby shower, but when you're pregnant at 16, it makes everyone very uncomfortable, and people don't wanna celebrate too much. They'd say congratulations with very concerned eyes, then quickly look at my mom in a way that conveyed sorrow.

Or they would just come out and say whatever.

I must've been eight months pregnant. We were at my sister's soccer game, and this woman walked up to me and my mom, looking at me with those sad eyes. Then while hugging my mom, the woman said, "I am so sorry!"

What is she sorry for? Who died? I thought.

Once Marc was born, I understood. But it wasn't until I held him in my arms, paralyzed with fear that I understood what everyone else was so scared about. They didn't believe that I could figure things out. So they looked at my mom with sad, sorry eyes because she'd have to pick up the pieces.

But I refused to let my dreams die.

Usually, when we look at kids, we see hope, potential, and dreams yet to be fulfilled. When most people looked at me at 16, with a baby in my belly, they saw the life growing inside me. But they also saw the death of what could've been, the death of my potential. They saw dreams failed before they even got a chance to be dreamed.

But I refused to let my dreams die.

When that lady hugged my mom and said sorry, what she was really saying was, "I am so sorry, Sloane's life is over. It will be so much harder, closer to impossible. She may never accomplish her dreams. I am so sorry that you are her mom, and you will have to deal with your daughter's shame and guilt. I am sorry that you are ashamed. I would never want to be in your situation. Thank God I am not you. I am so sorry."

Wow.

Truth is, she could've been right. My teacher also told me I could look forward to collecting food stamps when I turned 18. The school counselor told me that my only option for college was a community college. I lost friends because their parents thought I had something contagious (little did they know their kids had sex before me).

Instead, something extraordinary happened when I held my baby in my arms for the first time. Tears rolling down my cheeks, I held him tight and made him a promise.

"I promise you that I will never give up on my dreams."

I've kept that promise. I live my promise. And because of that, I never let my current circumstances define my future.

In fact, just the opposite happened.

I graduated from high school with honors and a special award from the principal. I received a full-ride scholarship to a private college in Hawai'i where I'd graduate with my Bachelor of Arts in Communications. I'd go on to become a professional actress and model appearing on over six network TV shows, and in ads and commercials all around the world. Then later, I stepped into my calling as an entrepreneur, coach, and professional speaker for over a decade.

Back then, I knew something those adults didn't. I knew that in order to be the best mom, I had to *show*

Marc that I could be the best me—prove to myself and others that my life wasn't over. That even though all the odds seemed to be stacked up against us, I wouldn't let those odds get the best of me. I knew that the only way Marc would have a future better than mine would be for me to live a life better than expected.

I was a girl who seemed to have the short end of the stick since I was little. I was sexually abused at 4, and I felt like I had no control over that. In this scenario, being a teen mom, I felt totally in control, in some odd way.

That is what I was able to do—control things. That, sister, is the answer to accomplishing hard things.

And the truth is, the ONLY thing you can control is YOU!

It starts with YOU!

You have to believe that You Can Do Hard Things. I am here to tell you that you can handle the hardest things life throws at you, despite what other people think. They don't matter anyway. You matter, and you can turn your hard things into beautiful stories of success and joy.

Only God truly knows how He designed me to make me this way. The strength He gave me, as broken as I was, to believe that I could travel down the road less traveled and tell this triumphant story...it's beyond understanding. It only makes sense because today, I'm able to speak this truth over others. Over you, right now.

It doesn't matter if I know you or not. It also doesn't matter if I know what you're going through. I know that you are not your current circumstance. You are more. You were made for more.

It's more than likely that you picked up this book because you are going through hard things, and you want some concrete answers. And if you aren't going through a hard thing now, you will soon (spoiler alert). We all experience hard shit!

Disclaimer

Most self-help books will promise you a road map to success. You won't find that here. I'm not gonna do that. In fact, I refuse.

What I am going to do is a far better solution. The saying is true, better to teach a woman to fish than to feed her for a day. I'm going to show you how to create your own road map to work through hard things. These are suggestions. Take the ones that work for you, and throw the rest away.

In the following chapters, I'm going to show you how I conquered hard things and how some other strong women did it too.

But throughout the rest of this book, I want you to remember that it all starts with YOU, boo!

It started when I was holding Marc for the first time. And the answer was simple: I can do hard things. All I can do right now is not give up on myself. That's the one thing as you decide to walk through your hard thing—you have to believe and you must believe in YOU.

Nothing's gonna stop me.

I can get through this.

Never give up.

I will find my treasure.

I can do hard things!

#NOTETOSELF

CHAPTER 4:

Goodwill Fishing Tales

"It's good to know where you come from. It makes you what you are today. It's DNA, it's in your blood." - Alexander McQueen

GOODWILL SUNDAYS

My mom would take me shopping at the Goodwill when I was a little girl. I didn't like the Goodwill, or G-dub as we called it. I hated the smell. To me, it smelled like if my great-grandma's closet ate an ashtray and turned it into a perfume and sprayed it over everything.

Yet, the Goodwill for my mom was and still is a treasure hunt that I benefited from every once in a while. I'll never forget those tap dance shoes I know my mom instantly regretted buying me. In my 7-year-old mind, I taught myself to tap dance. In reality, I was just driving my parents nuts.

The look on my mom's beautiful round face, that look of pure determination to find a piece of treasure and score a deal, is carved into my mind like the president's faces on Mount Rushmore.

Till this day, if you let her, she will spend hours combing through clothes and trinkets until she finds that exact thing she was looking for. I can hear her now, "Sloane, look, this is exactly what I've been looking for. I've always wanted one of these, and it's only four dollars!"

My mom is the most thrifty and resourceful woman I know. She can pair a G-dub top with a pair of leggings and look like a million bucks. Just the same, she can turn a can of pork and beans and spam into the most delicious meal you ever did have. Don't believe me? Come over for dinner! Her fried rice is famous.

We shopped at the G-dub and never went out to eat. My parents said no more than they said yes, but we did go on one family vacation to Disneyland when I was 12. The only other time I left the island was because my grandfather took me to the Big Island for a family reunion. It wasn't until I was in college that I finally visited other islands of Hawai'i.

My parents invested in our education. My sister and I were in private school, which I know wasn't easy for my parents financially. They saved up all their money to buy a house because they were young and on a budget. Going out to eat was a special event, I knew exactly what I was allowed to order, and never dared order anything else to drink besides water.

As I grew up, I'd see that look in my mom's eyes over and over again. That look that said, nothing's gonna stop me, we can get through this—You Can Do Hard Things!

The value of hard work

My parents taught me the value of hard work. My dad worked for the water company. He was up early and home late. When overtime called, we celebrated the fact that he'd be off to work again, pulling 24-hour shifts meant overtime pay, which meant less stress and may be a little more fun. I blame my parents for my workaholic tendencies.

Even though my parents worked a lot, we always had time for play. My dad, being a fisherman and hunter, always had my sister and me in the ocean or in the mountains. The ocean was my dad's G-dub, so to speak. He navigated the ocean with respect and confidence. We'd often go trolling. That's where you go far out in the ocean and bottom fish, slowly pulling your line for HOURS. My dad could stay out there forever if you let him.

I vividly remember trolling. When the reel would start spinning, pure adrenaline would shoot through my body. I'd grab my little scoop net, not that it would help, but just so I could feel a part of the moment. My mom and I would anxiously scan the ocean, waiting to see this huge marlin surface from the deep. My dad fought to reel in the biggest fish he'd ever caught, sweat dripping down his face. And that look, that same look in his eyes, just like my mom's. It was pure determination, a look that said, "Nothing's gonna stop me. We can get through this. Never give up. I will find my treasure—we can do hard things!"

My dad never caught that marlin. In fact, more times than not, his line would come up bolohead. That's a Hawaiian saying that means empty, like a head with no hair, a line with no fish. But my dad never gave up. Every day after school, when he wasn't working overtime, we'd load up the boat and head out for another 300-hour tour.

Whether we caught fish or not, it didn't matter. What actually mattered were the lessons I learned all those years ago:

Nothing's gonna stop me. I can get through this. Never give up. I will find my treasure. We can do hard things!

This has become my mantra, my attitude, my personal motto in life. It's what this book is about after all! It was etched into my soul and the foundation that helped me get through all the hard things I've experienced. It saved me when I was 16 and pregnant, and when I ended a physically and mentally abusive relationship. It helped me when I got a scholarship to attend college even though no one thought I'd even graduate from high school. It helped me when I started five businesses by the time I was 32, with no experience at all. And it helped that time I launched an online community and then sold it to one of the largest nonprofits in the world.

I was blessed that this motto that had been ingrained into my mind and heart as a young girl. My mission in writing this book was to dissect how you can apply it to your hard things. And I get it, a mantra and motto just aren't enough sometimes. The actual how-tos are what you really need.

For years, I studied this attitude of: "Nothing's gonna stop me. I can get through this. Never give up. I will find my treasure. We can do hard things." I've worked with hundreds of women from all over the world who are both challenged by this, yet are able to overcome the adversity they face with it. In unparalleled circumstances, they applied this motto we'll now call You Can Do Hard Things, and they realized a life free of not enough-ness, fear, and overwhelm.

I promise whatever hard thing you're facing, you will get through it. You need to, 'cause on the other side of your hard things, is your purpose and calling. And so many people are waiting for you.

OF COURSE THE EXACT HOW-TO'S

are important, but ultimately,

IF YOU DON'T HAVE CLARITY

on what you really want,

THE COURAGE TO THINK YOU CAN DO IT,

and the certainty to find solutions

to the problems along the way,

YOU'LL NEVER BE ABLE TO START.

CHAPTER 5:

Failing Forward Into Hard Things

"If you're not failing, you're probably not really moving forward." - John C. Maxwell

FAILURE IS A PART OF LIFE. I've failed more times than I've succeeded. In fact, I've failed my way to this very moment. If it weren't for all the wrong turns, I would not be here in my bed writing to you. I would not have had countless opportunities to use my gifts in the best way possible. So to all of my fuck-ups, I say, "Thank you! I honor you, and I can't wait for more!"

A mentor once told me, "Hang out with someone who has failed at what you want to do, and you'll quickly find out what not to do, which is far more valuable than the latter." He gave me this advice after I'd failed miserably on my own, but I never forgot it.

So that is my gift to you—my story of failures. May you learn from them, use them, and never repeat them.

The Boutique

In 2011, I had no money, but I was determined to open a boutique. My previous business experience came from running a cleaning business for three years. I was inexperienced and doomed to fail, but I did it anyways.

Maya Bella Boutique officially opened for business on May 16.

Freshly painted thick teal and white stripes lined the walls, seashells and starfish paraphernalia everywhere, and the clothes. Oh, the clothes. Be still my heart. This marked the era of my best-dressed moments.

The store smelt the opposite of an old man. It smelt like mermaids and unicorns and fresh cut wood. My heart pounded as I flicked on the lights and got the store ready for our first day in business. It felt like the first day of school. I walked over to the perfectly spaced garments, ran my fingers past each one, and picked the long blue and white striped maxi to wear for my first day on the job.

We had feng shui'd the place. Because when you take out a $25,000 loan, max out your credit cards, and close your other business that was actually making money to chase after your dream business, you do anything you can to invoke success. The checkout counter was facing the front door because according to feng shui, that was the optimal place so the money could flow in.

I counted. 10 ones, 5 fives, 5 tens, 5 twenties...

The air conditioner hummed.

I put the money in the drawer, closed it, and the world stood still for a minute.

I looked out the front door into the parking lot, and I instantly regretted it all.

What did I just do? This is insane! Can I really do this?

Is this what I really want?

You see the thing with moments like this is that they are very real.

They are not some kind of scene from that movie with Julia Roberts, when she leaves her fiancé at the aisle and runs away with her wedding dress on. Getting engaged and planning the wedding day feels like a fairy tale, and then BAM! The actual day arrives, and you're consumed thinking about what marriage really is, all that's involved, and the looming thought, *Am I really in love?*

That pretty much sums up what I was feeling. Except I had nowhere to run.

So, I said, "I do" wholeheartedly. I was all in!

I committed to the success of the store. As I write this, I'm smiling at my mental montage of cheering, deep conversations, huge shopping parties, beautiful clothes, and the faces of all the beautiful women I was blessed to meet and grow to know. All the love that flowed in and out of those doors was worth every moment of pain. The growth that I've had as a business owner, coach, speaker, wife, and mom, I owe to that store.

In under a year, the store outgrew the first location. I thought we had arrived. The new location was 2,000-square feet of retail space across the street from Whole Foods. I was paying almost $3 per square ft, plus common area maintenance fees, plus a percentage of the sales.

Oh, yeah, I also had three new employees, more inventory, more events, and more bills. Every month felt like I could barely pay it all. Even at our highest grossing five-figure months, there never seemed like there was enough money.

The art of resourcefulness

But I never gave up. I practiced the art of resourcefulness. It's something my dad taught me. My dad can do anything. I once watched him pull an old dirty engine out of the bushes and turn it into an actual running Jeep. If something broke in the house or on a car, he read a book and fixed it. And this was pre-YouTube, y'all! He built our house with his hands (and a few more sets from friends), but he did it all.

My dad didn't go to college. He didn't go to school to be a builder or mechanic. He was self-taught, and so was I.

I wanted the store to have an amazing website. I got some quotes and was astonished to find out that an amazing website would cost me over $5,000. Instead, I invested in a course that would change my life. I paid $2,000 over a year and learned to fish.

When the store was empty, I'd dive into the course. It taught me not only how to build a website, but also how to build a community, a tribe, and another source of income. I learned those skills out of desperation but based on the art of resourcefulness that my dad had instilled in me. Those skills would end up opening the door to opportunities I could've never imagined.

Learn to fish

The saying is true—better to teach a woman to fish, than to feed her for a day.

And I was fishing, y'all!

You see, my store was a safe haven for other women who were starting and growing their businesses. I wanted to feature local designers, so I was blessed to help some of these women launch and grow their businesses while growing mine.

But the thing was, as I was helping those women, connecting them to resources and each other on endless coffee dates and lunches, it got overwhelming. It seemed like everyone wanted to meet with me to pick my brain. I knew there had to be a better way.

Everything I was learning in the course was such perfect timing. To bring in extra money to the store, I'd host vision board workshops, networking events, meet the expert nights.

And one evening while I was hosting one of those events, I had an ah-ha moment.

What if I start an online community to host these

workshops virtually? After all, so many of my biz friends were moms too and couldn't be out on a Tuesday at a networking event at 8 p.m.

So I did. I launched the website, and with it, I launched an online community of powerful female entrepreneurs.

My first online business was born out of necessity, grit, and a whole lot of grace. After spending hundreds of hours with other entrepreneurs and having been one myself, I knew what we needed, especially as women chasing after our dreams. We just needed to hear, "You can do it too!" And the best way to hear that was through the stories of other women, just like us.

Of course the exact how-tos are important, but ultimately, if you don't have clarity on what you really want, the courage to think you can do it, and the certainty to find solutions to the problems along the way, you'll never be able to start.

So I went all in to develop engaging content for my community, so much so that it caught the attention of the Women's Small Business Administration in Hawai'i. And they wanted to buy my online organization.

Selling the organization was a hard decision. But I made it nonetheless. I was failing forward.

I decided to sell it to one of the largest nonprofits in America, and I was retained as a quasi-consultant to help with the merger. The merger wasn't pretty, and I learned a lot during the process. But in the end, it was a total God moment.

During that time, our retail space was also sold to the second largest commercial real estate holders in Hawai'i. That meant that rent was rising, and the bills of the boutique kept growing. I knew that a change was coming, and I was embracing for impact. But I didn't just want to take the storm on the cheek, so to speak. I wanted to get ahead of it. Like a storm chaser, I prefer to chase it rather than be chased.

I made a decision to pivot. Entrepreneurs often ask when they should give up. "When do you stop and move on?"

There isn't an easy answer because my take on this is contrary to popular self-help gurus out there who will flaunt the hustle harder mantra. I'm here to tell you that it's okay to change direction. That thing that you started may morph into something else, and more often than not, that something else is better than what you started with in the first place.

Pivot

I love the story of Sarah Blakely, American billionaire and inventor of Spanx. She set out to become an attorney, then went to work for Disney, tried her hand at stand-up comedy, and later sold fax machines and copiers door-to-door in Florida. And that's what sparked the idea of her now billion-dollar business. She was forced to wear hosiery in the hot Florida weather and decided that there had to be a better way. So she invented Spanx. Now that's a story full of pivoting!

I pivoted too. I turned the boutique into a co-working space. So I sold all the clothes and pretty things and turned Maya Bella Boutique into The Hive Hawai'i, the first co-working space on the windward side of Oahu. It was insane, and I had no idea what I was doing. It was my Hail Mary pass.

That was a total fail forward moment. It was a time for me to really discover what I truly wanted in life and business. And I share this story to show you that it's not a straight line to discovering what you really want.

There are two kinds of people in this world: those who were born knowing exactly what they want and those of us who have to discover it along the way. The thing to remember is that you have to be willing to take the risk, to fail over and over again to finally fall into your calling.

Regardless of which kind of person you are, you'll have moments in your plan where you realize you have no control over other people. Remember, it starts with you. And regardless, you have to make the call. Pivoting isn't about failure it's about solutions.

While the bills were piling up, I borrowed against the equity in my house twice. The second time was to re-brand and launch this co-working space. Everything was riding on the success of that new space.

My husband and I worked day and night to turn the boutique into a swanky co-working space with a phone booth, see-through doors, desks we made out of board and metal legs, chalkboard walls, and a dressing room area turned conference room.

We opened The Hive Hawaii to much fanfare. Newspapers and magazines wrote about us. I planned TedX style talks and networking events full of fashion, lots of wine, and productive networking.

Despite our efforts, we weren't getting regular revenue. There was still too much month at the end of the money.

After 3 months, we were drowning because the storm had caught up to us. So I planned our exit and started working with our landlords to try to get out of our lease. Breaking the lease meant we'd be on the hook for over $160k.

I'll never forget that day. I walked into the landlord's offices, holding back my tears and steadying my hands. I was going to ask them to let us out of our lease.

Who did I think I was?

All I knew is that it was my only option, and I had to ask!

While we were awaiting the landlord's decision, I made us an appointment with a bankruptcy attorney to see if we could save our only asset, our home, should things go south.

Kameron (my husband) at my side, we sat across the bankruptcy attorney, while he told us that because I was a personal guarantee on the business, our home would be listed as an asset and we could be forced to be put up for sale.

My heart stopped. Every feeling of shame and guilt came flooding in like a tsunami. *How could I do this to our family?* We left that meeting, sat outside a small coffee shop, and I couldn't stop crying.

What have I done? Lord, help me, please.

I've always been a praying girl, but I was like crazy praying girl during this time. I was talking to Jesus on the regular out loud in the Walmart, in my car, basically wherever I went. And I was making all kinds of deals with Him.

Lord, if you help me out of this, I will do anything!

Some people say God doesn't bargain. In my experience, He absolutely does!

The next day I got a call from our landlord, they were letting us out of our lease. It's only by the grace of God that we were let out of the lease with a measly $3,000 bill. A large supplement business agreed to essentially buy out our lease, freeing us of the $160k balance.

We had thirty days to move out, but we did it in under a week.

I stood in the middle of my empty store, my failed dream, feeling empty. I grieved what could've been. I cried. I was brought to my knees as if finally feeling the exhaust of the fight I'd been fighting. I ran my hands across the floor, remembering my husband putting in these planks with his bare hands, my eyes scanning the thick turquoise and white stripes that lined the walls, and I whispered to myself, "Your current circumstance is not your future. Get up, Sloane Ketcham. What's next? What do I really want?"

I turned over the keys and walked away. I grieved

for more days than I'd like to admit. I watched tons of motivational videos on YouTube and poured myself into every book and online course I could get my hands on.

There had to be more

You see, even though I'd closed the boutique, the co-working space didn't work out. I was confused about what I was going to do next, but I knew there had to be something more. I was confident I could get through hard things. There had to be a way. As an achiever and maximizer per the StrengthsFinder test, I wanted to get up fast. Faster than any other time before. (I recommend that test if you haven't already taken it.)

I spent many days at home on the floor of my garage, curled up in a ball, crying uncontrollably. I prayed, thanked God for his grace in this moment, realizing that the very floor I wept on could've been swiftly taken away.

I closed my eyes and rested in gratitude and asked God for a vision. It could've been minutes, but it felt like hours as my mind's eye danced from thought to thought. I remember being in such a state of surrender, I just let go.

That whole saying let go and let God—that's exactly what was happening. All of a sudden, out of nowhere, I saw an image of myself standing on a stage, looking out into a sea of people. I couldn't see their faces, no one was applauding, or reacting. They were just there, a faceless crowd.

I'll never forget that moment on my garage floor. That moment of pain gave birth to the beginning of a dream.

It's been quite the journey going from that garage floor to today, CEO of SloaneKetcham.com and the Speak Life Tribe. I serve women in life and business through a monthly membership, and later this year, I'll launch Speak Life International Inc. a global nonprofit that empowers women through microlending, mentorship, motivational and educational tools to start, grow, and scale their businesses. It's taken me years and lots of pivots to get where I am today.

That took a lot of kicking back those evil thoughts that would creep in...

Who am I to do that?

What would I do that hasn't already been done?

Why me?

I'm not qualified to do something like that.

Not today, Satan! I replaced those negative dream-killing thoughts with words of life.

Why not me?

Who am I not to do this?

I can do hard things!

Then I got up, wiped away my tears and tapped back into resourcefulness, reminding myself that I knew how to fish, and that it's okay to pivot.

Where are you?

Sis, there's always something more, and there's always something better. There's a Japanese proverb that says, "Fall down seven times, get up eight." If you're scared, not feeling like you're enough, possibly a little crazy from trying over and over again to no avail, it's okay. Or maybe you also have been cold, crying, and lost laying on your garage floor. Having cold feet should always be addressed before you take the leap. But sometimes when you get cold feet, you'll ask yourself if you're ready and the answer will be a resounding YES! And guess what. Things won't work out the way you planned, and that is okay!

Here's the truth—things never go as planned, they are always better!

You don't have to figure

anything out.

You don't have to seek anymore,
You don't have to look for any
answers or solutions.

Just let go.

Let everything go.

Surrender.

CHAPTER 6:

Surrender

"Surrender is a journey from outer turmoil to inner peace." - Sri Chinmoy

ONE OF THOSE massage franchises finally arrived on the island, and I swear I was the first in line to sign up for a monthly massage membership. I'm not joking! I was waiting outside their offices in anticipation because mama needed a massage. Plus I love a good deal. A massage for fifty bucks an hour and the first one was free?! Sign me up!

I remember the staff was cautiously impressed by my excitement. The sweet girl filling out my intake form was dressed in scrubs, probably hoping to give off a medical professional vibe. She said something like, "So, you must really need a massage, huh?!" She could tell I had some serious issues. I mean it's not like they were opening a Chick-fil-A and handing out free SKIMS (that's Kim Kardashians version of Spanx). Lord baby Jesus, help me if that ever happens.

You see, the thing was that I was convinced that this was going to be the answer to all of my problems. After all, I was practicing self-care and putting me on the to-do list (insert eye roll). I set up my auto pay, and my first three months of massages were scheduled in my phone calendar. I left feeling accomplished. I was busier than ever rebuilding my life financially, all the while stuffing my emotions in my stiff, knotted shoulders.

See, back in 2014, I had become a full-time network marketer. I was selling the American dream of quit your day job to seek residual income. It was a laptop-based lifestyle infused with free exotic trips around the world.

I had said yes to an opportunity with a brand new health and wellness network marketing company, and my team was growing exponentially. I had dabbled with network marketing in the past but never seriously. I'd buy nail art, random cupcake-flavored shakes, and Tupperware. But I didn't understand how people could actually make any real money at it until I was actually doing it. I noticed the biggest difference when I was consistently spending time around people making the kind of money in a single month that most people make in a year.

This particular company manufactured green juice products. Their flagship product was a 10-day transformation which promised to help you lose ten pounds in ten days. People were dropping weight like crazy—

some losing thirty plus pounds in ten days. The woman leading the launch of this company (and the top earner) was a friend who had been trying to recruit me into other companies for years. The timing had never been right for me until then.

The launch leader was fierce. A serial network marketer, and a master recruiter. She convinced me to give the 10-day transformation a try. And go figure, I lost almost twenty pounds. I was convinced. But if you want to know the truth, I wanted this to work so bad that I probably willed those twenty pounds to fall off my body.

But I saw the opportunity to be so close to the top of the pyramid. It's where I wanted to be. I needed a win. I was so desperate after closing my retail business. I needed to get off the garage floor because I wanted to be anywhere else but on that floor.

Being that I'd owned a boutique and had an online organization of female entrepreneurs, I had access to a list of women. Most of them seized the opportunity to lose a ton of weight. It required minimal effort and no exercise. The sign-up process was effortless.

Just a month after I joined her, I had blown threw the first ranks right into a leadership position as triple star Galactica ambassador. (I'm poking fun at multi-level marketing (MLM) leadership rank titles, but you get the point). I continued my rise to the top of the color-coded pyramid on the fancy PDF company poster. I broke company sales records in what felt like a whirlwind of successes. I was on my way to leading one of the fastest-growing teams in the company.

I was working harder than ever. My phone was permanently attached to my ear, while my arms would aggressively chop the air as if to tell my kids and poor husband to shush. Every family meal and outing was endangered by being interrupted by another very important call that I just had to take.

As my team of sales reps grew, so did my focus on everyone else but me and my family. *I'm doing this for my family, right?!* I had to make up for the failure of the retail business. In my mind, I had to do it at all costs, even if it hurt my family. I justified it all, convincing myself that one day they'd understand.

Obsessed with success

I was so obsessed with winning that I lost all sensibility and ability to set boundaries. Don't get me wrong, I loved what I was doing. Well, I didn't really love the whole health and wellness thing. I'll be 100 percent honest here—I was in love with the business of building a team and helping people to build businesses.

Over the next few years, that's what I did. And I did it wholeheartedly. Because the way the world of network marketing works, you can only get to the top by helping other people get to the top. That's how you climb the pyramid.

Every other month, I took planes, trains, and automobiles to do whatever I had to do to help my team win. As my team got bigger, the gap between those who were on their way to the top and those who couldn't get off the starting line started to widen. I was utterly exhausted. And cognitive dissonance started to creep in. I was frustrated with the fact that the definition of success in this business was like stuffing people into a box that they should never be in in the first place. I was stuffing myself into a box that I was not supposed to be in.

I got back from a whirlwind trip to Utah, where I had a team that was exploding. Entire families were joining. If this team did what most expected, I would reach one of the highest ranks in the company. I landed at the Honolulu airport, and instead of being excited at the potential, I was tired and numb.

I just need a massage

Just my luck, I'd pre-scheduled a massage for the day after I returned to Honolulu. Julie, the masseuse, was my favorite. She was a tiny Japanese woman, but her hands were strong. She never seemed to mind that I talked on the phone during our entire 90-minute massage.

But that day, things were different. I undressed, got on the table, and waited for her to knock on the door.

"Sloane, you ready?" Julie asked.

"Yup, come in," I said whimpering.

"You want medium or hard pressure today?"

"Whatever you want..." I replied, exhausted.

"You want your phone?"

I started to cry uncontrollably.

Julie started to massage me as I apologized to her profusely for my emotional meltdown. Then sweet little Julie saw her opportunity to hit me while I was down. She said in her thick Japanese accent, "Sloane, you my worst massage client, always talk on phone. You don't know how to relax, take care yourself. I glad you cry, it's okay."

I cried harder, thinking...*Julie, you are not my favorite anymore! Gosh darnit! I will show you Julie, I will not be your worst massage client. I will show you self-care!*

We never like truth tellers at first. But it's true that the competitor in me is relentless. I closed my eyes and sunk into the massage table like I never had before. I felt every muscle tense and release as if she was moving every one of my stuck emotions out of my body.

I surrendered

It was in that moment on the massage table that my healing journey began. It was in my moment of seeming victory that I had to surrender to the truth. I did not want to be a network marketer. I was tired of all the travel, and operating from a space of scarcity. I just couldn't figure out why more people weren't winning on my team. This isn't a book about network marketing, so I won't get into that here. But let's just say, I have very strong opinions. It was time for me to move on. It was time to pivot. Again.

I broke up with network marketing, but I'm forever grateful for the lessons I learned while we were together. And I never brought my cell phone into a massage again.

*FEAR'S NOT
SOMETHING TO
BE AFRAID OF.
WE'RE MEANT TO
EMBRACE IT,
FACE IT HEAD ON,
AND LOOK FOR
THE LESSON.
WHEN YOU FIND
IT, IT'LL BE YOUR
GREATEST GIFT.*

CHAPTER 7:

The Ifs And Fs

"Don't give in to your fears. If you do, you won't be able to talk to your heart."
— Paulo Coelho

AFTER ALL THE surrendering and pivoting, I went from nearly bankrupt to building a thriving business that helps others start, launch, and grow their businesses. I'm speaking and training on stages across the US, and coaching and training women from all over the world. I feel incredibly blessed.

Although, when I look back on it all, it feels like a bit of a tornado. I wanted to use the word whirlwind, but that seemed too nice. I told you from the get-go that I'd be honest. This process was not a whirlwind.

A what-if tornado

What's a *what-if tornado*, you ask? It's a new set of evil thought mongers that come flooding into your head like a tornado immediately after you get off the garage floor of failure, and they threaten to keep you down and destroy your new dream.

- *What if I fail again?*
- *What if this doesn't work?*
- *What if people think I've lost my marbles?*
- *What if my husband or family won't ever support me again?*
- *What if my kids resent that I work too much?*
- *What if I'm just not cut out for this?*

I've never been in a real tornado. One of my client's, Sharon, lives in a part of the country that is all too familiar with tornadoes. Actually, just a few weeks ago she survived one of the deadliest tornadoes in Nashville. She said it came with little warning. She was blessed that her home is an older house in the area and had a bunker. As the tornado hit, she and her husband immediately headed underground to take cover. The tornado passed over the top of them. She said it sounded like a steady ferocious roar combined with a raging waterfall that pierced your ears and shook your body.

National Geographic defines a tornado as

"a violently rotating column of air that extends from a thunderstorm to the ground. It's often portended by a dark, greenish sky. Black storm clouds gather. Baseball-size hail may fall. A funnel suddenly appears, as though descending from a cloud. The funnel hits the ground and roars forward with a sound like that of a freight train approaching. The tornado tears up everything in its path. Tornadoes can occur at any time of year, but they are more common during a distinct season. Tornadoes form when warm, humid air collides with cold, dry air."[1]

As she described it to me, I got this visual of the what-if tornado. A what-if tornado is exactly that. And just like an actual tornado destroys everything in its path, a what-if tornado will steal, kill, and destroy your dreams if you don't take cover.

- Have you ever been caught in a what-if tornado?

- Have you ever been so terrified to get back up and try again?
- Do the what-if questions have you paralyzed, or feeling stuck?

If so, here's my 2-step what-if tornado survival guide. Guaranteed to get you through any hard thing storm.

Step 1. Frame up your brain bunker.

Just like when building a house or bunker, your brain needs a frame to put up walls to protect you. You have to frame up your brain bunker to protect your mind from every negative what if. It's so simple, and will take you less than five minutes a day.

For every negative what if, you'll replace it with a positive what if. Write all your positive what ifs on a sticky note and put the note on your bathroom mirror or somewhere that you'll see it every morning. Read it out loud first thing in the morning, every day!

For Example:

Negative What If	Positive What If
What if I fail again?	What if I win?
What if this doesn't work?	What if this does work and I can finally live out my purpose and calling?
What if people think I've lost my marbles?	What if I didn't care about what other people thought about me or my dreams?
What if my husband or family won't ever support me again?	What if I'm no longer afraid of abandonment/rejection?
What if I'm just not cut out for this?	What if I was born for this?

Step 2. Face your fear.

Fear is the hardest to overcome. It's so hard. The phrase "fear not" is mentioned in the Bible eighty times! Therefore, I will not sugarcoat this step, and I refuse to use cliché quotes and Tony Robbins mantras for this step (although I love them).

It's horrible to imagine, but imagine if Sharon and her husband froze when they heard the tornado that was heading their way. Imagine if they just threw their hands in the air and gave up. When the sirens went off, they were afraid, terrified in fact, but they had a plan. They were prepared and did what they needed to do to stay safe. That's how you kick fear in the ass.

It's fear that'll convince you that those negative what

ifs are real. It's fear that'll have you believing that you can wait till tomorrow, or the next day, or the next year to start your dream business, career, or ask your cute co-worker out on a date.

I know fear all too well—I've faced her time and time again. But there's one time in particular that stands out when I think about facing my fears.

Iraq

By the time I was 26, I had gone through some pretty doggone hard things. But I had fallen into such a rhythm of simple and good.

Kameron was a private in the Army and I was an aspiring realtor. We were living on ends meet, raising our 11-month-old daughter and 7-year-old son. We had the cutest apartment that overlooked a bar and gas station, which made people watching from the balcony with a glass of wine a cheap Friday night date. Kameron's family lived only three and a half hours away, so we'd hop in our car on long weekends and holidays to soak up family time. We were blessed.

Then, a cold day arrived in November 2009. Kameron was leaving for Iraq. There we were in a tiny room filled with families, babies, men, and women in uniform, waiting to say goodbye. Fifteen months in Iraq. You could cut the anticipation, fear, and agony with a knife.

As luck would have it, Kameron was terribly sick. He had a fever and felt like he had the flu. I was so pissed, "Seriously, now of all times, you are going to get sick?!" *Fucking great timing, buddy!* Obviously empathy is not my strong suit.

It's funny what fear will make you do or make you turn to. I was angry on the verge of rage.

Truth was, he didn't have the flu. He was riddled with fear. Throughout the whole three months leading up to deployment, he had decided to bottle up his emotions and keep everything inside. Almost to a point that I had thought he wanted to go to Iraq. I was so confused by his calm demeanor and nonchalant regard for the fact that he was going to war. Our fear had shown up differently. For Kam, it was physically in his body. For me, I became angry and super emotional.

I remember sitting in that tiny stinky waiting room, looking at the women in my husband's unit, and feeling torn and super confused by the thoughts racing through my mind. On one hand, I was grateful, as I could not imagine having to leave my kids to go to war. On the other hand, I was devastated for them. I also felt resentful, and my fears of being abandoned came racing back. I thought, *I want to go somewhere for fifteen months away from mommy duties and the realities of life.* The fear of this moment had me stuck in all the what ifs. I bounced right out of reality and into a total what-if tornado.

Fear is real

It was time. Kam looked at me, his face was totally pale, and he quietly said it was time for them to get their weapons and line up for formation. I had heard the busses pull up. so I knew it was true.

As he got up to get his things together, he looked at me and said, "Don't worry, it's not time yet. We just gotta grab our weapons, and then we'll say goodbye." As if prolonging the inevitable would somehow make the goodbye easier.

As I watched my husband sling his weapon over his shoulder, I thought, "Will he have to use that?" Up until that point, he'd only ever shot at targets and an animal here and there.

.   .   .

And that's when I felt it. I fully felt the reality of the situation. That this may be the last time I would ever see my husband, ever again. Nothing was in my control, and I was terrified and paralyzed. You know how people say fear stands for *False Evidence Appearing Real*? It's dumb. When people say that, my eyes roll so far back into my head.

It was at that moment that I knew there is nothing false about fear. Fear is real, but what mattered most was how I was going to choose to react to it. *How would I face this thing called fear?*

His platoon stood in their final formation and their sergeant said some things that no one cared about, and then allowed them to say their goodbyes before getting on the bus that would take them to the airport.

As Kameron walked up to us, our son was crying. He picked him up, held him tight, and told him that he'd be home soon and asked him to be helpful. He kissed our daughter who was just learning to talk, and told her to behave for me (she's our strong-willed child). Then, without skipping a beat, he grabbed my hand, pulled me close, and said whatever he had to make himself feel better. Something like, "Don't worry, I'll be fine. I'm going to be safe. It'll go by fast. Before you know it,

I'll be home." We hugged, kissed, and then I watched as he got on the bus.

For the next fifteen months, I lived in total fear. I'd watch the news and hear about soldiers dying, and cry for what felt like hours for their families. I ate more, I slept less. My real estate business was doing well, I worked harder than ever to take my mind off being worried.

Some would say I was a complete mess. I turned to more wine (seems to be a theme), more news, and more crying. I went to the doctor for my annual checkup, and she simply asked me in a cheerful upbeat demeanor, "Mrs. Ketcham, how are you?" I proceeded to cry like a baby. She looked at me, scribbled on her pad, and gave me a prescription for antidepressants, which made me even more depressed.

I could feel myself spinning out of control.

Letting go of fear

I had all these fears running around in my head. One night I put the kids to bed, curled up with my favorite bottle of merlot, turned on the TV to watch the news, and something came over me. And I immediately turned the TV off. Instinctively, I knew that first things first, I needed to stop watching the news. All of it was the reality of war, and people were losing their lives. I could not do anything about that.

I was terrified that Kameron would not come home, or he'd make it home with a missing leg, or arm, or both or paralyzed. When the fear of what if gets so big, so sticky that you're stuck in it, the only answer is to face it, head on.

How to face your fear

I don't know what you're afraid of or what you've been dealing with, but I know you can conquer your fear! We all have fears—some small, others big. Whether it's starting a business, writing a book, having a baby, or going off to war, uncovering where that fear actually comes from is the key.

It's like weeding a garden. My friend Marcy coaches children's book authors, and she once described the book writing process to me like weeding a garden. She said, "Sometimes you have to write a bunch of stuff that you'll eventually never use, to uncover the fertile soil that lies beneath."

. . .

When she said that to me, I thought about this process of facing your fear. It's the same thing! Thank you, Marcy!

In facing your fear, you have to dig through the weeds, remove the small and big rocks, and the thorny covering to uncover the roots. That's when you can find out what's really holding you back.

Fear keeps you small by tangling you up in the weeds. I was afraid that Kameron wouldn't make it back home to me and the kids. That fear was very real and valid.

But as I started to expose those weeds and rocks, the root of all the fear was exposed. Most people want to cover up their fear. In fact, most people do. In this situation, it was the first thing Kameron and I did—him with avoidance and me with anger and resentment.

My husband's story is his to tell. I will say that the man who went to war is not the man who returned home to me and the kids. So in a way, my fear did become reality. For years, he was worse, and it's only been in the recent years that I have seen a new man emerging. I am proud of him and the work he's committed to doing.

I'm grateful for his and every other service member and their families' sacrifice. Let us never forget.

Fear's not something to be afraid of. We're meant to embrace it, face it head on, and look for the lesson. But listen, we have to find our way. What I did may not work for you, so do that 30 percent thing by reading and listening, soak up what you will, and throw the rest away.

The Face Your Fear Foolproof Plan

Here's my Face Your Fear Foolproof Plan.

Step 1. Weed your fear garden.

Start by asking yourself what are you afraid of in the form of a what-if question, and don't stop until you get to the roots. For example, when Kameron went to Iraq, this is what came up for me.

- What if he doesn't come home, and I'm all alone?
- What if I'm not a good mom alone?
- What if I can't do this by myself?
- **I'm afraid to be alone.**

- What if I can't survive this?
- What if I'm not a strong enough woman, wife, or mother?
- **I'm afraid I'm not enough.**

I had to untangle all those weeds and deal with each fear one at a time. These aren't as simple as replacing them with a positive what if. Although, it does help, and you should definitely do that! These fears required deep healing and lots of therapy that I still do as part of my "work" today.

What are your what-if questions? Are you wanting to start a business? Finally start healing? What fear is holding you back?

Step 2. Soar with eagles.

Fear wants to keep you isolated. You being alone with your fears is never a good combination. You need to find other people who you can trust that can support you, and who you can support. However there are criteria to build your eagle flock.

· · ·

DO NOT seek advice from people who have never gone through what you want to do, who are naysayers, and/or highly opinionated, often starting sentences with, "What you should do is..."

DO seek a circle of support from people who have accomplished a level of success that you look up to, people who are positive and ask a lot of questions.

When Kameron was in Iraq, I was building a few businesses. I was a part-time realtor, while hustling to start a cleaning business on the side. (Weird combination, I know. But hey, remember we all pivot.) I met a group of entrepreneurs, and we formed a mastermind and called our group The Eagles. Till this day, we meet once per month and annually for our Eagles year-in-review session. My Eagles have seen me through every business win and loss and many personal highs and lows. They've helped me face my fears by encouraging and challenging me, by asking me all the tough questions, all the what ifs. We've been soaring together for almost a decade now, and I know the best is yet to come!

Step 3. You can't try to sit in a chair!

Facing your fears isn't something you give a try. I heard a mentor on a coaching call once, and she told her client, "You can't try to sit in a chair, you're either gonna sit down or you're not!"

At first I thought, "Geez, that was intense." Then I lol'd as I imagined what that would look like if I tried to sit in my chair. Facing your fear is exactly like that. You have to commit to the process and do it. You either sit in the chair or you don't. It's up to you. And trust me, sometimes I choose to not take a seat, and that's okay. You have to take it one fear at a time.

As I'm writing this book, all kinds of fears come up, but I committed. I'm sitting in the freaking chair! According to various sources on the world wide web, about 97 percent of authors never finish their books. I totally get it. I know why—it's all the fears.

Sit in your chair, sister!

Your

Vision

is your

Victory

CHAPTER 8:

The You Can Do Hard Things Fail-Proof Formula

"If you bring forth what is within you, what you bring forth will save you. If you do not bring forth what is within you, what you do not bring forth will destroy you." - Gospel of Thomas

LET'S put this all together. So far, we've determined that this is your moment to step into your calling. We've unpacked your calling and the misconception that once you find it, the skies will part, and unicorns will appear; instead, we now know that #thestruggleis-real and more times than not, your calling is born out of pain. We discovered that your real power comes from turning that pain into your purpose so that you can help others to transform and change their lives for the better. We unraveled what-if tornadoes, faced our fears, and let them GO!

"Now what?" you ask.

I hear you, girl!

I've come to know over my years of working with hundreds of people that the only thing that separates those who achieve their dreams and those who don't is courage and imperfect action. It's not the person who is the smartest or who is more naturally talented. Nope. The differentiating factor is YOU, sister!

It's you, the girl who's willing to do the hard things!

And because it's you, I'm so excited to share this. This is the moment in the book where I get to I lay out the *You Can Do Hard Things Fail-proof Formula.* And when I say fail-proof, I mean it. I set the foundation for this formula when I was 16 years old, and then perfected it over years of failing forward over and over again to come out with the win!

When Kameron left for Iraq, I dove deep into personal growth and professional development, head-first actually. Some may have called me obsessed. But I didn't care, I wanted to be better, to do better. And there was something inside of me that knew I was made for more. I was in my mid-twenties, I had three kids at that point, and we were a military family. But I knew that we wanted something different.

Kameron didn't want to make the military a career —it was always a means to an end for him. And I hated the moving, unpredictability, and lack of control we had over our lives. When Kameron left for Iraq in 2007, I was pursuing a real estate career.

Then, the market took a nosedive in 2009, shortly

after Kam returned. Beyond the crazy market, I was dealing with all the things that come with love and war, kids and a career. Kameron decided that it would be a great time to stay home with the kids and focus on them and me full-time. Thank God for my husband.

I started to read a lot of books. I decided that I'd go through the entire first page of Google for the search phrase "classic personal development books." I committed to reading fifteen books, one for every month that Kameron was in Iraq. I ended up reading sixteen.

Here's a list of the first books I read:

- *Think and Grow Rich* by Napoleon Hill
- *The Magic of Thinking Big* by David J. Schwartz
- *How To Win Friends & Influence People* by Dale Carnegie
- *The 7 Habits of Highly Effective People* by Stephen R. Covey
- *The Power of Now* by Eckhart Tolle
- *Do The Dao Now* by Dr. Wayne Dyer
- *Rich Dad, Poor Dad* by Robert Kiyosaki
- *The Alchemist* by Paulo Coelho
- *The Power of Positive Thinking* by Dr. Norman Vincent Peale
- *Awaken the Giant Within* by Tony Robbins
- *The War of Art* by Steven Pressfield

- *The Four Agreements: A Practical Guide to Personal Freedom* by Don Miguel Ruiz
- *Conquering the Financial Kingdom* by Dani Johnson
- *The Art of Exceptional Living* by Jim Rohn
- *The Richest Man in Babylon* by George S. Clason
- *The Psychology of Selling* by Brian Tracy

All these years later, I still read one book a month on average. Every book then and now gives me something new—a new perspective, a new vision, or a new habit. Books have a tendency to challenge your view of the world. They can give you a glimpse of what is possible beyond what you can immediately see.

Even though I always had the attitude of You Can Do Hard Things, it wasn't until I started studying the power of the mind that things began to change. I began to understand that thoughts are things in their own right, and that influences how we change.

This realization made my life's vision come together like pieces of a puzzle that were previously just dancing in my head. I was able to really start dreaming because I was creating a vision for my future. I would not have dared to dream of owning my own businesses, writing books, becoming a coach, and being able to help women from all across the world. Before I started implementing this formula, I would've never imagined being able to own our dream home in Hawai'i. I owe it all to this formula. It gave me the courage to pursue my calling, and that's my hope for you!

On any given day, you can find me teaching this to clients, friends, or your friendly grocery clerk check out person. Here's one of the best parts—this formula has worked for people from all over the world, from Abu Dhabi to the UK, South Africa to Australia, back to the US and home in Hawai'i. It also works for people from all different backgrounds and socioeconomic status. That includes those who are launching businesses and projects in roles ranging from authors to health care workers, personal development coaches to real estate professionals, marketing gurus to educators. The list goes on!

And the very best part is that this formula is so simple. You'll find yourself doing it in the carpool drop-off line, as you scan the aisles of Target, and while sipping your fav-oh glass of vino. This is not some silly confidence-building exercise—it's proven to help make dreams come true.

STEP 1. Turn your vision into victory. Visualize.

"Where there is no vision, the people will perish" *Proverbs 29:18 (MEV)*

"What you perceive, you receive" - *Many gurus*

It was 2016. Kameron and I sat on the front porch of our brand new home in Hawaii, only a stone's throw away from the Pacific Ocean. We had just finished unpacking, salty air blowing through our hair, while we sipped on our favorite glass of pinot. We said cheers to twelve years of marriage, full of gratitude as we watched the sun dip behind the gorgeous orange and pink horizon. Our dream had come true.

It's so crazy to think that just seven years prior, we were living in Washington State while Kameron was in the Army. We rented this cute house in a town called Dupont, right off the military base. When I say it was cute, I mean it was tiny. But we made it ours.

One scorching Washington summer, Kameron found a HUGE waterslide on Craigslist and went out to the Walmart to get the most significant blow-up pool he could find. At the time, I was very pregnant with Kanekoa, our youngest son, so that pool was *everything*! Kameron set up our own little Hawaiian beach in our Dupont backyard. It was heaven.

I'd spend what felt like hours, but was probably more like minutes, visualizing what going home to Hawai'i would look like. The saying is correct—there's no place like home, and I wanted to go back. I wanted to raise my babies with a real beach in their backyard. I wanted them to grow up knowing my parents and family, our culture, the aina (or land in Hawaiian).

That entire summer while I attempted to float in our Walmart pool, in my mind's eye, I'd built our Hawaiian dream house. Board by board, room by room. I could see, smell, and hear the ocean. I'd imagine Kameron and I sitting on our porch, toasting to a good day as the sun falls behind the horizon like we do now.

Giving birth to a vision

While in Dupont, I spent a decent amount of time lying in my Walmart pool, staring at the clouds, and drifting into my daydreams. I'd visualize my baby, his birth, and exactly what I wanted it to be like. We wanted this birth to be unique because Kameron was able to be there. Kameron adopted Marc when he was 7, and unfortunately, Kameron was at basic training when our daughter, Kaleia, was born.

Kanekoa was born at the end of that summer. Not to brag, but the nurses said she had wished they'd recorded his birth so that she could show other women what a delivery could look like. What can I say? I'm an overachiever.

I gave birth naturally with the other two, so of course, Kanekoa's birth plan was no different. I want to be clear here, this isn't a story of "Who gave birth better?" I'm very aware that you may have had a complicated birth story or chose to get the epidural. Sister, if that was you, it's all good! That's not what this story is about.

You see, Kanekoa's birth meant so much to me. This would be the one and only time I didn't have to bring a life into this world alone, overwhelmed by fear and worry. When I gave birth to Marc, I was 16. When I had Kaleia, Kameron was away at Army basic training and wouldn't meet her until she was about 3 months old.

So, for the first time in my childbearing years, I was

about to have that Instagram-ready #werehavingababy moment with my amazing husband by my side.

Kameron was so excited to be there. Although he didn't get to do any of those things that husbands do in the movies, he was the perfect partner. All that visualizing worked. There was no yelling or screaming, just peaceful Hawaiian music in the background, a stillness in the room, and the anticipation of finally meeting our baby boy.

I had spent the entire summer visualizing that very moment, from the socks I was wearing to the way my hair was braided. I'd lie in that Walmart pool and visualize exactly what I'd do when a contraction started. Breathe in, breathe out, relax, sink into the pain, deeper into the pain, breathe, release, relax. I had done it so many times that in the hospital bed, it was like second nature. I was aligned—mind, body, and soul. I felt totally prepared and in control. I was in labor for about eight hours and pushed three to four times until Kanekoa Lee Ketcham made his grand entrance.

Your vision is your victory

How'd we have such a good birthing experience? Don't go running to Walmart. The magic wasn't in the pool.

The magic was in my mind's eye. I saw it and believed it before it was actually in existence. Then I repeated that vision, much like a song on repeat, over and over again.

Vision is the first step in the *You Can Do Hard*

Things Fail-proof Formula. It doesn't matter if you're literally having a baby or starting a business, which often feels like the same thing. You have to start with a vision.

Your vision will prepare you for the moments that get tough because trust me, things will get tough. Contractions and expansions in life will come, you will face ups and downs, and lefts and rights. But if you have a vision that is big, bold, and comes from inside of you, when the pain hits, you'll breathe in, breathe out, relax, sink into the pain, deeper into the pain, breathe, release, then relax. You'll go on the ride, you will commit to the journey, you won't fight it, you'll embrace the fear because you will know that right on the other side of it is your victory.

I've created a few exercises that will help you to deepen your visualization muscles. I've been doing this exact process for over a decade. You are going to love it!

Vision Exercise

1. Visualize your ideal day. What does your life look like in your ideal day? What are you doing from the moment you wake up till the moment you go to bed? Write it out in the present tense and be as detailed as possible. I give you permission to dream. (In my day, I added a chef who cooks us dinner!) Then record it as a voice memo on your phone or computer. Play your ideal day recording back to yourself at least first

thing when you wake up and then as you are falling asleep every day.

2. Create a vision board of your ideal day, split up your board into four sections: Family, Health, Finances, and Community. Then put it somewhere that it's readily visible every day.

3. Share your vision with a trusted friend.

STEP 2. Emotionalize Your Win.

"The best and most beautiful things in the world cannot be seen or even touched. They must be felt with the heart." - Helen Keller

"Whatever the mind can conceive and believe, it can achieve." - Napoleon Hill

Once you've done your vision exercises, you're ready to move into step two. Unfortunately, this is the step that most people skip. If visualizing is the process of getting your mind into tip-top dream-manifesting shape, then emotionalizing your win is getting you out of your head and into your body, dropping your vision into your gut and straight into your emotions so that you can literally change your state of belief. The ultimate goal is to move from visualization to certainty.

Have you ever wanted something so bad that you just knew you were gonna get it, and that it was only a matter of time? I remember when we were buying our first home, I'd found it online It was a short sale, and it was perfect. The house was also on the same street where Kameron and I had met just three years earlier. I called our agent at the time and told him to write up an offer for $50k less than the asking price. I heard him gasp. He asked me if I was sure, and I was. There was something inside of me—that still quiet voice—that knew this house would be ours. For months, we didn't hear a word. I continued to do my visualization exercises and increase my belief. I allowed myself to get excited and feel what it would feel like to walk into this home. When I closed my eyes, I visualized our home. I imagined Thanksgivings and Christmases and lazy family movie nights, and I allowed my emotions to take over. I felt joy and happiness and love as if it were real in that very moment.

It doesn't matter if you want to increase your revenue ten times over, start your dream business, or finally write that fantasy novel, the process of emotionalizing what you want will help to break through to your subconscious mind.

Your Subconscious Mind

Your subconscious mind is like a huge memory bank. Its capacity is virtually unlimited, and it permanently stores everything that ever happens to you. By the time you reach the age of 21, you've already permanently stored more than one hundred times the contents of the entire Encyclopedia Britannica.

Your subconscious mind works day and night to make your behavior fit a pattern consistent with your emotionalized thoughts, hopes, and dreams. Your conscious mind is the driver, and your subconscious mind is the pilot, simply obeying. Your subconscious mind grows either flowers or weeds, whichever you plant. It doesn't discriminate between the two.

Emotionalizing the vision you have for your life is like tending to your garden. Emotionalizing is positioning your visions in your subconscious mind's most fertile soil so that it has the best access to the sun and rain. That helps it to grow and flourish without obstruction.

John Assaraf is the founder and CEO of Neuro-Gym, a company dedicated to using the most advanced technologies and evidence-based brain training methods to help individuals unleash their fullest potential and maximize their results. He says, "Once an idea is chosen and consistently impressed and emotionalized onto the subconscious mind, perceptions and behaviors change to find and produce the desired results."

Whenever I'm setting a new goal or casting a new vision, it's this part of the *You Can Do Hard Things Fail-proof Formula* that I look forward to the most. This exercise is meant to be done quickly, frequently, and consistently. Emotionalizing is the process of celebrating your win before it has actually happened.

Emotionalize Exercise

1. Visualize what you want, your dream, or your goal. Close your eyes and see it as if it were real. Identify three emotions that are

coming up for you as you imagine achieving your goal.

2. Take those three emotions and complete the following sentence with each. I feel _____ because _____.

Here's an example:

My goal is to complete an ultramarathon.

I feel **proud** because **I see myself crossing the finish line.**

My goal is to write a book.

I feel **AHHHmazing** because **I'm finally doing the thing I've always wanted to do**!

My goal is to launch my coaching business.

I feel **fulfilled** because **I'm pursuing my purpose in life and helping people do the same.**

Step 3. Action, Action, Actualize.

"The path to success is to take massive, determined actions." - Tony Robbins

"An idea not coupled with action will never get any bigger than the brain cell it occupied." - Arnold Glasow

"God provides the wind, but man must raise the sails." - St. Augustine

The last thing left in the *You Can Do Hard Things Fail-proof Formula* is to take massive imperfect action on your calling. There's not much to explain here except to say that nothing happens without action.

If you've done steps one and two repeatedly and

with certainty, the how and what will reveal itself. I don't mean to sound all mystical here. It's simply the truth. One of the biggest mistakes I see people make is that they get started with this step. Obsessing over the plan, how they're going to launch their thing instead of laying the foundation first.

If you've visualized and emotionalized, the actualization is a natural byproduct of your subconscious mind nudging you to take action on your new beliefs, and in total confidence. Your faith may waver from time to time. But hey, you only need a mustard seed anyhow, right?! Keep going back to your vision and tapping into your emotions, you'll find the courage to pursue your calling.

Sister, if you want a step-by-step plan to take action on your calling, I created this resource page just for you. I know there are gonna be some of you who are ready to take action today. You'll find my courses, Start the Right Business, Launch Your Online Business, Goal Setting 101, Marketing 101, and so much more! I wanted to give you some free resources to help you get off to a great start. Visit www.sloaneketcham.com/YCDHT free to get a move on!

Beautiful Girl,
You Can Do
Hard things!

CHAPTER 9:

Beautiful Girl,
You Can Do Hard Things

"You can't just sit there and wait for people to give you that golden dream. You've got to get out there and make it happen for yourself." - Diana Ross

WHEN IT CAME to launching my coaching business, I was going to create my ideal life. I was ready to ask for what I wanted. I felt different, unapologetic. I refused to be driven by money and notoriety. Instead, I was driven by my moment of surrender and what I really wanted.

All the personal growth and development tools were screaming at me loudly, asking me, "What do you really want? Whatever you want, you can have. You just have to ask and believe."

What I really wanted was to help women build

their own success stories. I wanted to help them create a life of meaning and purpose, where money would not be the end-all be-all, but a byproduct of stepping into their highest and best use. Diddy said it best with his warning, "Don't chase the paper, chase the dream."

But I had one problem. Even though I was crystal clear about the business and life I wanted to create and I believed that I could do it (I'd been doing it for years already), I couldn't shake feeling like an imposter. All the years prior I hid behind other brands or businesses. This time, I was stepping out as me. I was the business, the brand, the courses, the content, the everything. It was me I was selling. I kept asking myself, *Am I enough?*

Imposter syndrome

My favorite movie of all time is *When The Jetsons Meet The Flinstones*. If you have not watched this movie, I am very disappointed in you. Please leave now and order it on Amazon. It'll be the best $1.99 you've ever spent. And you are welcome.

This movie is especially helpful if you've ever been stuck in imposter syndrome. The Jetsons are a family from the future who end up traveling to the past in their time machine. In the past, the Jetsons meet the Flinstones. Enter conniving villains and chaos, and the families accidentally end up switching lives. The futuristic Jetsons are stuck in the caveman era where the dad, George Jetson, ends up building a bunch of businesses in the Flinstone's town of Bedrock, all the while secretly paranoid that the town will find out he's a fraud and futuristic. Meanwhile Fred Flinstone, the caveman dad, is now in the future feeling totally out of place, but everyone is so intrigued by him that they somehow make him famous. (Stay with me—it's a cartoon.) Both George and Fred make the best out of their situations. In fact, they end up winning big time before being sent back to their original eras.

In business and in life, sometimes you have to go to places where you don't feel like you belong. When I was starting my new business, there was a part of me that felt a little like George Jetson and a bit like Fred Flinstone. I was stuck in the past building something new all the while feeling a bit like an imposter through it all.

The trick is to just keep going. You're going to feel out of place starting something new. You're going to feel like you don't belong. But it's okay because You Can Do Hard Things.

If my crazy Jetsons and Flinstones example didn't work for you, just remember Tony Robbins. Tony is another great example I love to use. When Tony started his career as a trainer and speaker, he was still cleaning offices at night and sleeping in his yellow VW bug. He really knew what he wanted and wasn't about to let his current circumstances get in the way of his calling. And you shouldn't either!

So, what do you really want?

When I ask women, "What do you really want?", 90 percent will answer with a knee-jerk response of "Hmmm, I don't know." Then I knee-jerkingly reply, "Sure you do!"

I've found that women are conditioned to dream politely. 'Cause sisters, let me tell you, when I ask men this question, 90 percent will answer the question the first time. What is up with that?!

Girl, you do not need permission to get what you want. You do not need to apologize for the desires in your heart to create something big and bold that no one's ever seen before. If it's in you, you are already qualified. If you can dream it, it is already possible. And if you don't have it yet, it's your job to keep moving toward it.

It's already been done

Can we agree, right here right now, that giving up is not an option? Here's when it's especially not an option. Let's say you're scrolling through the Facebook, and you see that your friend just shared her friend's new business, and just so happen it's exactly what you wanted to do. In fact, it's what you've been thinking and dreaming of doing for years. So, you click the post and enter into the world of giving up.

NO! You are not allowed to give up on your dream.

This is the moment you lean in, work harder, and build bigger. The real Truth (with a capital T) is that there is nothing new. If you are thinking of inventing something, the odds are someone else is too. The differentiating factor is that you are YOU. With your own unique set of skills, powerful voice, and bubbly personality, the world needs YOU.

Before we took tests in grade school, the teacher would have us put up folders so that our neighbors couldn't copy our answers. When you get distracted, put up some freakin' folders, keep your eyes on your own assignment, get a little mad, and burn the dang boats.

Burn the boats

I get it. Taking action like that is super scary. But when you decide that it's time to pursue the calling on your life, there's no other option. If you've never heard this saying before, you might think I'm starting to lose it. Allow me to explain.

There was this fierce and slightly reactive Spanish captain named Hernán Cortés, and he went in search of treasure in the early sixteenth century. The queen gave him six hundred soldiers, sixteen or so horses, and eleven boats for his quest.

When Cortés arrived on the island with the supposed treasure, Cortés did the unthinkable—he burned all of his boats! He set the things on fire, y'all!

Can you imagine being one of his soldiers and watching your boat go down in flames? *Okay, boss, message clear. There is NO turning back! We either win, find the treasure, or we die.*

Long story short, they won, conquered the Aztec empire, and found their treasure. Let's be super clear, my point with this is to emphasize the determination of Cortés. I definitely don't condone his ruin of the Aztec civilization.

What boats do you need to burn?

Your boats may show up like negative relationships, *Real Housewives* reruns, and or your own stinkin' thinking. Or maybe it's finally time for you to leave that job you hate? I don't know what that is for you, but I'm cheering you on. And I will be dancing with you at the bonfire. Burn those boats, baby!

Every year I make it a goal to attend one live in-person event. I do that because the first live event I ever attended changed my life. It's the reason this girl from a small town on the North Shore of Oahu, who became a mom at 16, is able to live out her calling, change lives, and pursue a life of passion and purpose. I was able to see what was possible.

I somehow always have older friends and a group of them in their mid-forties (at the time) invited me to go to their company's convention. I was 25, bright-eyed and bushy-tailed, eager to accept the invite.

My friends worked for an insurance company, and every year this company flew speakers in to motivate their sales team for three whole days. I told Kameron about this event with sparkles in my eyes. Even though I had no idea what it was about, I could feel it in my spirit. I just had to be there. Being the ever-supportive husband that he is, Kameron immediately said, "GO!"

Problem was, we had no extra money for such frivolous things. But as God would have it, one of my friends offered to let me stay in her hotel room. All I needed was a plane ticket. I scrounged miles from my mom, put twenty dollars in my pocket, and I was off. Thank the Lord the hotel had a free continental breakfast!

The kickoff morning was like nothing I'd ever experienced. Pulsating music, upbeat base vibrating the floors, people jumping up and down at 7 a.m.. There was something indescribable about being in a room full of people so full of excitement. The collective consciousness somehow was seeping into my soul and changing my insides...or I was being brainwashed. Till this day, that's still up for debate.

The days were packed with world-renowned speakers like Bob Proctor and Jack Canfield who all were seemingly saying the same thing: "You can do anything," "The impossible is possible," and "If I can do it, you can too!"

And I was buying it all, hook, line, and sinker.

By the last day, I was about to become an insurance agent. I still didn't know what they actual sold or how the heck to do it, but whatever it was, whatever I was experiencing at this event, I wanted it FOREVER. I wanted to put it in my jeans pocket and take it home with me forever.

And then he took the stage. Les Brown, the keynote speaker, was the man in charge to land the plane, and this was a big plane might I say. Those highly motivated insurance agents filled a football arena. The friends I was with were the top team for the entire company, so we had front and center seats.

When Les took the stage, I swear he winked at me. I leaned forward, knowing whatever he was about to say, he was saying it to me. I was right, right along with 50,000 other people. There was something about sitting in the front row, and till this day, I do my best to get that seat. I try my hardest to sit in the front even when I feel uncomfortable or shy about it. If the seat is open, I take it, and I encourage you to do the same. The experience in the front row is pure osmosis.

Les started, and the crowd hushed. But as he progressed through his 90-minute speech, his cadence quickened, his demeanor changed, and the crowd got louder. He went beyond what every other speaker over the last three days had done. They were there to teach and train. Les was there to change lives. He shifted the atmosphere. He took us into wild unapologetic possibility.

I was overwhelmed. Something came over me, and I felt like I was in church. You know when the pastor gives a sermon, and it feels like he's talking right to you, like he's reading your mind. Yup, that feeling.

I looked around me to check if anyone else's face looked like mine, I wondered if anyone was thinking what I was thinking. No one was looking back at me. Everyone was standing in agreement, shouting AMEN. He was asking the crowd over and over again, "Are you hungggry, ARE YOU HUNNNGRRRYYYY?!"

Everyone shouted in unison, "YES!"

I was hungry, literally hungry. But I also wanted to shout back, "NO, I'M STARVING!"

I was starving. I wasn't just hungry for change and meaning and purpose and clarity and passion—I was starving for it. And then I had my come-to-Jesus moment. Every cell in my being realized that what Les was doing, I was being called to do too. And the moment I felt that, in that exact moment of knowing, I heard a voice whisper in my ear, "Who do you think you are? You are just a small town girl. No one will listen to you. Sit down!" So, I sat down defeated and confused.

Les didn't stop. Why would he? There were 50,000 other people to cater too. He gracefully moved into his closing as I sat back in my seat, about to give up. "The graveyard is the richest place on earth, because it is here that you will find all the hopes and dreams that were never fulfilled, the books that were never written, the songs that were never sung, the inventions that were never shared, the cures that were never discovered, all because someone was too afraid to take that first step, to keep with the problem, or wasn't determined to carry out their dream. Friends, my challenge to you today is to live full. Live fully so that you may die empty."

I jumped up. Everyone was on their feet. Confetti fell from the ceiling, and I promised myself in that moment that I would do just that. I'd live full, die empty. I challenge you, Beautiful Girl, to do the same.

You Can Do Hard Things! You can tell that devil of doubt on your shoulder to shut up and get out because you have work to do. You have been called for such a time as this!

Final words

Beautiful Girl,

Before you leave, I want you to know that you are a warrior. You are brave and bold. I know it hasn't been easy. There will be days that you will wish the world would stop so you can breathe. But it won't.

People will tell you that you can't do this or that, and you'll feel like your dream is slowly dying. Do NOT believe them! Do you hear me, sister? Do NOT believe them!

Here's the Truth (again with a capital T): there are things you can't do, so you will have to ask for help. It will be hard. But asking for help is the only way to get to where you want to go.

You'll learn to trust. That will be the hardest, and there will be a lot of people who will let you down.

But remember, your current circumstances no matter how bad they may seem, do NOT define your future. There is a plan for you, and it is a mighty plan. BELIEVE THAT!

As you walk through life, people won't understand the choices you make. Please, please, I beg you—do not care what other people think of you. They do not matter. All that matters is what you think of yourself. Cultivate your confidence. You may need to borrow some from time to time, and that's okay. Borrow it, then give it away freely when it's someone else's time of need.

Every day your life begins anew. Every day you have the permission to dream. There is a call on your life, and you owe it to you and the world to answer that call. Don't be selfish with what God has given you.

Your unused, neglected, and hidden gift will eventually waste away. Sister, do not waste your gifts. Now is not the time to hide. YOU are needed, your voice is needed. Trust me, I know that your calling is like a dare to walk into the wilderness, but you are not alone. Yes, your path will be harder than most. But that just means you'll have a more adventurous story to tell. You'll fight harder, you'll dig deeper, and your legacy will live on longer. When you get tired, and you feel alone and want to quit, remember this: you're doing the hard things, those things are the right things, and those are the things that matter.

Beautiful Girl, You Can Do Hard Things!

Xo,

Sloane

NOTES

7. The Ifs and Fs

1. https://www.nationalgeographic.com/environment/natural-disasters/tornadoes/#close

Acknowledgements

To God, be the glory. I will praise you all the days of my life. Thank you for carrying me through the wilderness.

My husband, we've been through so many hard things, all the hard things, and here we are learning and growing through it all. I'm proud of us, and I know the best is yet to come. Thank you for holding my hand, being my biggest fan, and loving me unconditionally through it all. Thank you for wiping away my tears, reminding me to have fun, and loving me well.

My parents, for raising me to be me, for teaching me all the skills I needed to get through and accomplish hard things, and for always putting us all first. Thank you for always being there for me, no matter what. You've taught me about love by showing me what it looks like.

Marc, thank you for lending me your story. You're a big part of this book. I pray, one day, you'll tell the world your story and inspire others with your vision, tenacity, and huge heart. Thank you for being my motivation and for bringing out the best in me. I love you, bubba.

Kanekoa, thank you for being my word counter. Thank you for reminding me to play, laugh, and smile. Kanekoa, you are a brave boy, and I pray we raise you to be a strong man of God.

Kaleia, my sweet baby girl, this book is for you. Thank you for being my greatest teacher. I pray that you unapologetically follow your calling, that when you are faced with hard things you remember, beautiful girl, you can do hard things!

When I was writing *Beautiful Girl, You Can Do Hard Things*, there were many days I didn't think I had it in me. I cried and rebelled, but I was blessed with a few friends who wouldn't let me give up on this dream, they loaned me their confidence and courage, and for that, I am forever grateful.

Jenna Clarke, for loaning me your gift of belief and hope. For always being there for me, unconditionally, every step of the way. You are my true champion. Thank you for trusting me, and encouraging me with faithful words and wisdom.

Tamra Leilani, for always telling me the truth with fierce love and wisdom. Your strength is beyond words. The day we met, I knew you'd be stuck with me. Thank you for pulling me out of my bat cave consistantly and for always reminding me to keep it real.

Kelly Bouchard, my coach, thank you for always speaking life over me, challenging me, and loving me through it all. Thank you for giving me the space to step into my calling, graciously allowing me to stand on your shoulders, there are no words to adequately express my gratitude. I thank Jesus for you.

My Eagles, Charlie, Marcia, and Jeremy, for holding me accountable and challenging me to believe beyond what I could see.

My connect group, Tanya, Hinano, Charmaine, Kau'i, Roz, and Meri Mine, for fighting in the spirit with and for me. Thank you, Jesus, for my sisters, not needy, but needed.

Edwina Reyes, my Therapist, for helping me to enter into *the work*, the hardest of all hard things, you continue to walk with me on this journey of healing, in partnership with the Holy Spirit. I am grateful to God for you and the work you do for me and so many others. Without your support, these words would have not made it to this page.

Geralyn, aka Mary, for our endless talks about life, spirit, faith, hope, and love. Thank you for inspiring me to always find the love even when it's messy, and for seeing me exactly as I am. I will never forget that moment at the Ko'olau Ballroom.

My coaches at Self Publishing School, Gary, Marcy, Lise, and Lisa, without your wisdom and encouragement, this would not be possible. Chandler and Omer, thank you for believing in this small town country girl. I'm a living proof that leverage impact is real.

Max, my emotional support dog. I know you can't read, but I could not write thank you's without including you. You came into my life and stole my heart. Thank you for making me a dog mama.

And last, by not least, to you, the reader. Thank you for reading my book. Thank you for braving your hard things. I hope we meet one day. I pray that you step into your calling with courage and unwavering faith, I pray that you turn all that pain into purpose and that YOU will be the reason, someone says, "If she can do it, so can I!"

About The Author

Sloane Ketcham is a speaker, coach, entrepreneur, wife and mom of 3. Known for her relatable approach to breaking down tough challenges and empowering women to connect with their life's calling, she speaks from a place of deep love and strength forged in the face of adversity. With a formal background in business and communications, Sloane has been mentored by widely recognized experts in personal and leadership development across multiple industries.

She is the founder of Speak Life International, a non-profit, whose mission is to help women and young girls change the world one story at a time through education, entrepreneurship, empowerment scholarships and micro lending.

"I'm not a superhero. I don't wear a cape. I was not born with a silver spoon. I don't come from privilege or wealth. I'm just an ordinary girl who beat the odds repeatedly. I believe we all have the power to do the same. We can do hard things!"

Blog: www.SloaneKetcham.com
(Click on "speaking" to inquire about having Sloane
speak at your event)
Facebook: www.Facebook.com/sloaneketcham
Instagram: @sloaneketcham

GET THE

You Can Do Hard Things

CRASH COURSE FREE!

As a gift to help you get the most out of this book, sign up for the crash course today! The Course will help you to implement faster, have deeper breakthroughs and crush your hard things with ease!

Crash Course Includes: Audio Book, Study Guide & Mini Course

Sign up by visiting:
www.SLOANEKETCHAM.com/YCDHT

Made in the USA
Columbia, SC
06 December 2020